THE AUTHORITY GUIDE TO
ENGAGING YOUR PEOPLE

Raise staff performance and wellbeing, increase profitability and improve customer satisfaction

SUE MITCHELL

The Authority Guide to Engaging Your People

Raise staff performance and wellbeing, increase profitability and improve customer satisfaction
© Sue Mitchell

ISBN 978-1-909116-84-9
eISBN 978-1-909116-85-6

Published in 2017 by Authority Guides
authorityguides.co.uk

The right of Sue Mitchell to be identified as the author of this work has been asserted by her in accordance with the Copyright, Designs and Patents Act 1988.

A CIP record of this book is available from the British Library.

All rights reserved. No part of this book may be reproduced, stored in a retrieval system, or transmitted in any form or by any means, electronic, mechanical, photocopying, recording or otherwise, without the prior written permission of the publisher.

No responsibility for loss occasioned to any person acting or refraining from action as a result of any material in this publication can be accepted by the author or publisher.

Printed in the United Kingdom.

Contents

Introduction	v
1. Why engagement matters	1
2. Leadership to engage your people	7
3. Meaning – purpose, values, vision	25
4. Listen – *really* listen to understand	29
5. Communicate	37
6. Working to strengths	43
7. Coaching	49
8. Understanding mindset	55
9. The power of positive	63
10. Understanding motivation	73
Resources and references	81
About the author	85

> Nothing destroys a person's or a team's energy, enthusiasm and engagement more than a negative attitude, which festers and spreads dissent widely so everyone suffers.
>
> Gallup, *State of the Global Workforce* White Paper

Introduction

Have you ever been sitting in an office where it seems like everyone is complaining? Miguel thinks the management are out to get him. John says he can't respect his manager and doesn't know why he got the job, he's not competent. Leila says she went on a training course last week but doesn't dare try anything out in case she's told off for doing things differently and being blamed if something goes wrong. Rebekka says she hates working here, it's so negative and demoralising. She's wondering whether she should find another job, but maybe it's better to stick with what you know. At least she can walk to work, do the minimum you need to get by and have a life outside work.

Have you ever worked in an organisation with a silo mentality, where highly competitive teams work against each other, not sharing information that would help another team be more effective? Or where cliques contribute to tense relationships and some people seem to get special privileges? Or where people are afraid to take any decision themselves?

In contrast, have you experienced a workplace where everyone is totally committed to what they are doing? They want to deliver their best work and know they are making a difference.

They talk about how they can work better together and share information to more effectively deliver progress towards the common goals – so there is no repetition or delays waiting for another section to do their part. They look out for what they can do to make improvements, feel confident to take decisions relating to their role and feel proud about their organisation. Working with them is a great experience for colleagues and customers. The difference comes down to engagement. It never happens by chance. Engagement fundamentally depends on your mindset as a manager and leader, influencing how you behave with others and how you design strategy, systems and processes. This book gives you insights and practical tips to engage your people and make the difference for your team and organisation. Additional tools and resources are available on my online resources page for each chapter to help you implement the ideas.

1. Why engagement matters

What is engagement?

Engagement is emotional commitment, which happens when:

- You have a positive emotional state, which is more likely when you experience wellbeing and are not stressed.
- You feel personally motivated to give extra value in terms of your attention, time, energy, focus, quality of work and so on (called investing your discretionary effort). You want to do what it takes to work to the best of your ability, deliver results and create value for your organisation. You work smarter and offer ideas and solutions to problems that you encounter.
- You have high job satisfaction and fulfilment.
- You have confidence in the organisation's future and believe in what it is doing.

As a result you become committed to the organisation and a loyal advocate for its products, services and as a place to work.

Why engagement matters

Repeated global surveys by Gallup find that engagement strongly raises performance, yet the 2013 Gallup report, *State of the Global Workplace*, found that worldwide only 13 per cent of people are actively engaged in their work. Most employees, 63 per cent, are 'not engaged' while 24 per cent are 'actively disengaged', meaning they are unhappy and spreading unproductivity, negativity and dissent within the organisation. In the UK only 17 per cent of employees are engaged, 57 per cent are not engaged and 26 per cent are actively disengaged. That's something every business professional should want to address and make sure that their organisation stands out as one of the few where everyone feels proud to work and is highly engaged. The difference is not only a great place to work where you enjoy what you do and being with colleagues, but also higher performance, higher productivity, higher customer satisfaction, higher staff satisfaction, reduced turnover of staff with consequent savings in costly recruitment and development implications, fewer poor quality incidents and fewer safety incidents. Over many years, across countries, organisations and thousands of employees, the Gallup surveys consistently show that organisations with high engagement strongly outperform those without, and have earnings up to four times higher than their competitors.

Engagement helps business to drive growth, be more resilient and succeed through periods of change, uncertainty and turbulence. In a special report for the UK government, MacLeod and Clarke (2009) showed that engagement can unlock productivity and transform not only organisational performance but also people's working lives, especially when a commitment to employee wellbeing and engagement is brought into the core business strategy. In their review on organisational wellbeing, Jeffrey and colleagues (2014) reported that focusing on wellbeing brings engagement and also raises creativity, innovation, productivity, loyalty, customer satisfaction and performance. The pace of change in the world increases year on year. Now is the time to engage people in your business so you all pull together in the same direction. Identify your opportunities, focus on what you can do best, and make it possible for your people to bring all their capabilities and skills into work, feel proud to work in your business and help your business thrive.

Your business can't survive without people, whatever the nature of your work, the kind of organisation or size of business. Sole trader to global corporate, local charity to international non-governmental organisation, engineering or technology to arts or therapies – ultimately your business needs people in order to thrive. (Even if you are the only person in your business, you need to engage yourself, your customers, your suppliers and your extended team – accountant, PR and so on.) When you inspire your people to be engaged with their work, they make your business great. Conversely, when you actively disengage your people, they can break your business – are you aware of how your actions and behaviour influence how the people around you feel?

How do you engage people?

Engaging people is about inspiring positive mindsets and changing the behaviour of every person so that the cultural norm is positive. To engage your people you need to create a positive environment and a culture of trust and responsibility where people can thrive.

- Provide personal resources, organisational resources and infrastructure that people need to excel in their role. Personal resources include recognising the knowledge, behaviour, skills and mindset that a person has and also investing in learning, coaching and development to support him or her to have the attitude and capabilities to excel now and in future.

- Ensure that activities stimulate positive mindsets and release each person's full potential as well as improving overall well-being. The most important activity is leadership behaviour by line managers and senior leaders for inspiring a compelling vision, trust and good communication – especially listening and acting on the information.
- Ensure that activities prevent stimulation of the threat centre in the brain (Chapter 9) including strategy and changing organisational processes to remove obstacles and frustrations. This is especially critical to think through during periods of change, which can threaten many core motivators at once (Chapter 10) and destroy engagement.

Barriers and obstacles to engagement are not just lack of engagement drivers but also different factors, that cause job dissatisfaction (see Chapter 10). In their large-scale survey on engagement in 2015, PwC report that increasing deliberate activities that raise engagement and intentionally reducing obstacles to engagement leads to higher productivity as more engaged people spend more days actively making progress towards the common purpose.

Key drivers for engagement

- *Leadership behaviour* sets the tone at the top for company direction and culture. Leadership behaviour by all managers, especially immediate/line managers explains a high proportion of engagement in organisations across the world. The relationship with their manager is one of the commonest reasons people give for leaving a role. (Chapter 2.)
- A compelling and motivating *vision*:
    o gives meaning and purpose to your work (Chapter 3)

- o gives confidence in the company, where it is going and its future, and a feeling of job security and pride in working for a successful company.
- *Trust*: research by the Institute of Leadership and Management (ILM, 2014) revealed that levels of trust within the organisation drives engagement: trust in leaders and managers, as competent role models with trustworthy intentions; trust that leaders have in those they lead; and trust among peers and within teams. Trust leads to healthy working relationships for effective collaboration and cooperation. Essential behaviours include being open and fair, communicating effectively, being able to make decisions, and showing integrity and competence.
- Inspire *cultural norms* throughout the organisation of what is accepted behaviour.
- Clarify company *core values* with which everyone can identify (Chapter 3).
- Effective *communication* (Chapters 4 and 5).
- *Respect and fairness*: everyone is treated well and with respect, whatever their role, background or ethnicity. There is no favouritism (Chapters 4 and 10).
- Work to *strengths*: develop people's strengths and match roles to strengths to raise motivation and performance as people do what they do best (Chapter 6).
- Provide *growth and development* opportunities: support people to develop competence and achieve career aspirations to reward intrinsic motivators (Chapter 10).
- Commitment to *quality and cooperation/collaboration*: promote excellence and good working relationships, and make it easier to work effectively across units to reward intrinsic motivators (Chapter 10).

- Perform regular engagement *surveys and act* on the information: listen from the top (or as the organisation) and act on what is working and what needs changing to encourage much higher active engagement throughout the organisation (Chapter 4).

- *Responsibility*: promote self-management, decision making and a sense of control in work, even if only subtly within the confines of each job's parameters, to raise motivation through autonomy (Chapter 10).

- High-quality frequent *interaction with line managers*: these may be quick check-ins and rapid team catch-ups (20–30 minute meetings, often remote). Use a coaching approach (Chapter 7) for high-quality interactions. Many managers focus on discussing tasks mainly from their perspective or hold one-way briefings, even in one-on-one meetings, which are not engaging. Make time to ask about your team member's perspective, thoughts and concerns, not just on this task but on wider issues.

- Sincere *commitment in core business strategy* to enhance wellbeing for everyone in the organisation.

- The above drivers are drawn from: Gallup, 2013; Kouzes and Posner, 2012; MacLeod and Clarke, 2009; PwC, 2015; Strycharczyk and Elvin, 2014; Thomas, 2009.

2. Leadership to engage your people

Jim Collins (2001) and his research colleagues demonstrated that great leadership is essential for long-term business success and for organisational wellbeing. According to research by Joyce and colleagues (2004), good leadership can raise performance by 15 per cent but poor leadership hinders performance by an equal amount.

What is leadership?

The trouble with leadership is that it is a complex, emergent property (to borrow a phrase from statistics) and highly context dependent. There is no simple, direct property that wholly describes leadership, or a few simple behaviours that you can always do in every situation. Which is probably why so many models try to simplify leadership and no one model can wholly capture it. However, there is still value in leadership models as they give you a starting point and a framework to think about different aspects of leadership in different contexts, and to begin to make sense of the complexity so that you can choose appropriate leadership behaviours for the situation you are experiencing.

Leadership is a paradox – you are least aware of it when it is done well, as was captured by Lao Tzu in about the fourth century BC: 'A leader is best when people barely know he exists. Of a good leader, who talks little, when his work is done, his aim fulfilled, they will say: we did it ourselves.' I think this paradox underlies the frequency of poor leadership being cited as reasons for poor performance in so many organisations, despite the centuries of study into leadership.

Leadership has thousands of definitions. My definition is: 'Leadership to engage your people is inspiring others to want to give their best performance to deliver results and achieve a common purpose.' It is not just about getting everyone behind a common purpose or vision and delivering results, but creating the culture and environment that:

- gives everyone the resources and infrastructure they need to play their part well; and
- inspires followers who are personally motivated and choose to give their emotional commitment to it.

I once heard a first violinist being interviewed on the radio about why their orchestra's conductor was so special, when it is the musicians who actually produce the music. She said other conductors were good, and kept the orchestra together and in time, but she loved working with this conductor as he did so much more for the orchestra to create an exceptional performance. He helped her to interpret the music in ways she had never thought of and drew from her a performance she never knew she had the ability to do. This conductor was leading in a way that totally engaged her.

Leadership is context dependent

Leadership is about the relationship between a leader and followers who are inspired by a common purpose. Even when you are leading a group, a team or a whole organisation, your leadership happens not at the group level but in your relationship with each person. Work at the individual relationship level to engage hearts and minds. *Make it personal.*

The nature of the leadership relationship is shaped by the context in which it happens – not just the person but also the situation. What one person needs from you in one context may differ in another context, and in any given situation, different people will look to you for different styles of leadership. I regard context as having two layers: an outer layer representing wider contexts that are not likely to be under your direct control; and an inner layer representing contexts you can directly influence in yourself and in your relationships, whether you are a leader or a follower. The outer context layer could include things such as the economy, technology, faith and culture (political, societal, organisational, community, family, etc.). The inner layer is influenced by the outer layer and could include things such as the group's attitudes, values, ethics, motivation, sense of purpose and level of trust in the relationship between leader and followers. This inner layer can be strongly influenced by your leadership style, whether intentionally or not. Many organisations' culture and way of working reflect the leadership style of the CEO and other senior influencers or leaders.

You are more effective when you match your leadership style to suit the context, particularly the wider context. For example, Churchill was an excellent leader for keeping morale high and providing a strong sense of purpose during the Second World War, but his style didn't suit a post-war Britain with different needs, a different purpose and different direction.

Who is a leader?

The other trouble with leadership is that many people think leadership doesn't apply to them or is only for people at the top of the organisation. Many small business owners and managers in small organisations have told me that directly. That's a dangerous myth and can be doing untold damage to their business' performance. Even if your business has only you in it, leadership is still relevant because no business operates in a vacuum. You have relationships with clients, customers, suppliers, your accountants, lawyers and other stakeholders and the better you lead them in a way that engages them, the more loyal advocates you will have promoting your business. Also, you are not your business, so you need to consider your relationship with your business and how it satisfies what you personally need from work to feel fulfilled, motivated and engaged. The better you lead yourself, the better your business will be.

Leadership is relevant at all levels throughout the organisation and the more you encourage it the more effective your organisation will be. Leadership is relevant in all walks of life, not just in work. For example, parents hold a vital leadership role as they influence their family and children's development, core values, attitudes and beliefs.

How do you 'do' leadership?

Leaders are, above all, expected to deliver results. However, it is the way in which you deliver results that determines the level of success. Unlike many subjects, where you gain knowledge and then do whatever is involved, because leadership emerges from your relationships with other people, there is also a critical element about how you are 'being' with people (of which many even senior executives seem unaware).

This is why people talk about being on a leadership journey and find there is a large overlap between personal development and leadership development. Perhaps because leadership is intangible, many organisations expect it will just come naturally once a person is promoted, and don't give sufficient (or any) training, coaching or other development. However, this sets them up to fail because they work using their previous expertise and often continue to focus on and value outputs and what to do – business needs, projects, tasks, outcomes, KPIs, results, deadlines, schedules and so on. Great leadership needs to consider not only the required tasks and outputs, but also individuals and the dynamic of the team or group of individuals, so they can work together harmoniously (see John Adair's Action Centred Leadership model (1973; there are many good resources on the Internet) and the higher dimension scales in the ILM72 model, see step 8).

Know about leadership covering both mindset (being) and the types of activities required to deliver results. Gain expertise in leadership in parallel to your technological/operational/practical expertise.

Be a leader. Have the right mindset: values, beliefs, purpose, attitude, responsibility, motivation, confidence, emotional intelligence, mental toughness, interpersonal skills, personality and so on.

Do leadership. Perform the actions and behaviours necessary to deliver results effectively within the context. Focus attention on:
- tasks – projects, organisational functions, delivering results, operations, strategy
- individual needs – recognise personal motivators, strengths, aspirations, support required
- team needs – build relationships, how we work together, communication styles, embrace differences, remove barriers (see Figure 1).

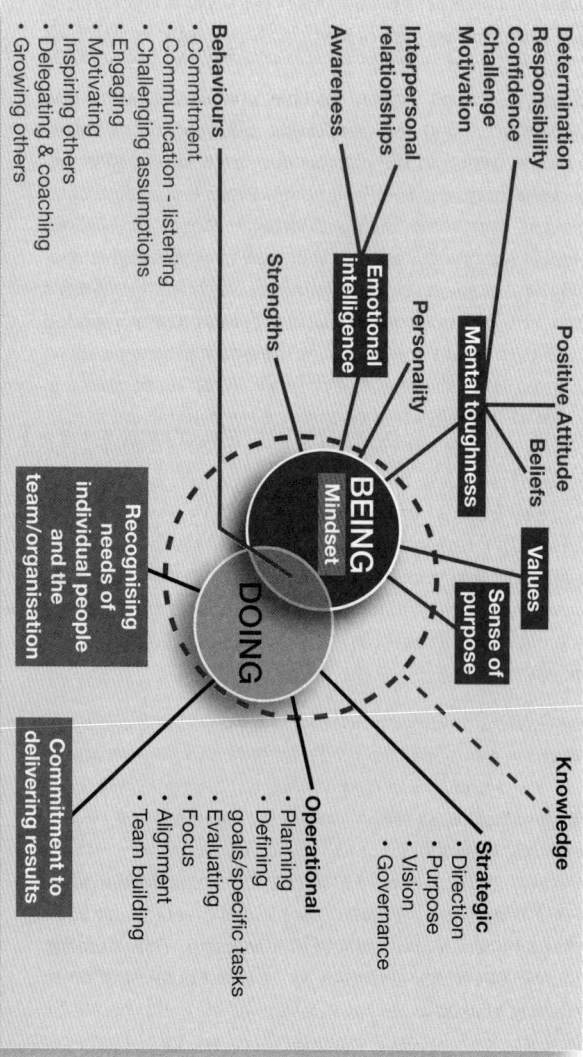

Figure 1 Knowledge underpins how to be a leader and do leadership activities.

Leadership behaviours make the difference for engagement

In repeated studies across multiple contexts, Kouzes and Posner (2012) found that leadership behaviour consistently accounts for much of the difference in levels of engagement. These behaviours align well with the 'Level 5 leadership' characteristics, discovered during extensive research by Collins (2001) and his colleagues into what makes organisations sustainably, highly successful. While the research was conducted on Fortune 100 companies, Jim Collins (2001) has implemented the 'Good to Great' principles successfully in organisations of all sizes, from micro to multinational. When leadership first came out of the analysis as the number one determinant of success, it wasn't believed, because it didn't match other research where leadership was found to be often important but not always critical (such as the extensive research by Joyce and colleagues, 2004). However, follow-up analyses revealed that the style of leadership in sustainably, highly successful companies was very different from that in the other companies. It is not just good leadership with a vision, but Level 5 leadership that makes the difference.

Level 5 leaders may not be well known outside the company, and may be ignored by the media as they don't fit the charismatic, 'newsworthy' leadership model, but they are well recognised within the organisation. Collins (2001) states that Level 5 leaders are highly ambitious for the company (rather than for themselves) and focus on a purpose for the common good, surround themselves with great people and create a culture of trust, determination and distributed leadership. They demand high quality standards and have the grit and determination to do whatever it takes to deliver excellent results in the long term, supported by an unquestioning belief it can be done, no matter what setbacks occur. Because leadership is so distributed, and the leader credits other people in the organisation for successes in the company, outsiders and the media cannot see any direct causal link between this leader and outstanding results, so do not recognise the essential impact and drive this leader has on the organisation's performance. This is a classic example of Lao Tzu's paradox.

Level 5 leadership elicits high engagement, and the good news is it can be learned. The first steps are to raise your awareness to truly know yourself and your people, and develop a high-performance mindset to connect with and engage your people.

10 leadership steps to build trust and engage your people

1. Know yourself and what you stand for

It is vital to actively notice where you focus your attention and know who you are and how you impact other people, so you can make better choices about how you act and interact with others. Awareness is essential to enable you to inspire others to want to work towards your common purpose, meet or exceed standards and deliver high performing results. Awareness is at the core of emotional intelligence and significantly raises your leadership capabilities, as reported by Goleman (2000) and many others.

Clarify and identify your:

- values (Chapter 3)
- purpose (Chapter 3)
- vision (Chapter 3)
- strengths, skills and capabilities (Chapter 6)

- beliefs and mindset – how do you view and interact with the world? (Chapters 8 and 9)
- motivations – what drives you? (Chapter 10)
- energisers – what raises your energy levels? What do you find renewing and refreshing?
- default communication styles – listening (Chapter 4) and communication (Chapter 5).

Use profiling tools to learn more about yourself and how you come across to others, and gain insights in how you compare with the general population. These give you a framework to assess a) what is working well for you and apply that learning in other areas, and b) what you might want to change and how you can do that. When you do this as a team, it gives you a common language to talk about issues that are often not discussed. It can transform how teams work together as each person gains new perspectives on conflicting situations and realises that at least some of it, if not all of it, comes down to different perspectives and ways of being and it is not personal. There are many useful profiles for leaders and it is better to choose one that has been widely researched and proven to be valid and reliable. Three that are particularly useful for you to improve how you engage your people are Emotional Intelligence (e.g. EQ-i2), Mental Toughness (MTQ48) and personality profiles.

Clarify your top three to five projects or initiatives and personal learning or development goals. Recognise what you need to stop doing to allow time to focus on priorities and learn how to say 'no' constructively to distractions.

Build time in your schedule for regular reflection for:

- learning from what is going well and what could be improved
- awareness of your impact on others and quality of relationships

- improving your ability to make rapid decisions by looking over the horizon. Mentally rehearse potential scenarios so you can respond appropriately.

Manage your energy so you spend more time doing things that are energising rather than energy draining. Do something renewing every day. Identify how you can integrate life and work to raise the quality and fulfilment you feel in all domains, rather than purely 'life–work balance' either/or thinking, which inevitably involves more trade-offs by trying to separate the two realms. How can you give enough energy and attention to important realms in your life to avoid stress and burnout?

Identify the important relationships in your life and at work and consider how you will nurture them.

Identify personally meaningful ways to celebrate successes.

2. Repeat step 1 to get to know and understand your team and your wider organisation

Build stronger relationships with all members of your team by getting to know each other more deeply and create the foundations for an exceptionally high performing team that harnesses the power of diverse perspectives, accepts differences and works to each person's strengths and motivations. Implementing mental toughness profiling and development with staff at all levels gives a framework for raising engagement and building a more resilient organisation (Strycharczyk and Elvin, 2014).

Build in regular team reflection sessions, in a positive, informal setting to:

- reconnect with and enhance commitment to the common purpose

- recognise what has gone well or not as expected and how to apply learning from that elsewhere
- provide an opportunity for everyone to share objectively their perspectives, good and bad, in a blame free environment
- improve team bonding and relationships.

3. Assess alignment between your personal and the organisational perspectives

Compare what you discover in steps 1 and 2 for yourself, your team and your organisation. What common ground can you find? What is not aligned? Find shared values between you, your team and your organisation and choose behaviours as a team to uphold, in order to work more effectively together. The more aligned you are around core values, beliefs and purpose the more you can engage others and inspire them to do the same. The more diverse your team's strengths are and the better you are all able to embrace difference constructively, the stronger your team will be.

As a leader, the more you are a role model for core values and are consistent in what you say and do, the better people can believe in you, have confidence in you, trust you and be more engaged (see step 5). How well do you 'walk the talk' and model desired behaviour for others to follow? How consistently do your actions reflect the organisation's values, standards and purpose? What message does that send to your people? What are the consequences? What do you want to do about it?

Where are your ambitions focused? Do you have sufficient ambition and aspiration for the common purpose? More than personal ambition? If not, what will it take for you to genuinely feel you can put the common purpose first? It will transform how well you can engage your people to get involved and get behind the vision and purpose.

4. Build your team

When you have the chance to choose who to have in your team, or if you are recruiting, consider who will be a good match for working with you and in your organisation. Jim Collins advises in *Good to Great* (2001): 'Get the right people on board the bus, and then get the right people in the right seats.' Match the role to the person, so each person is working to their strengths.

Develop a team charter that covers how you will work together to deliver results, including the team's purpose, why it is important and elements from step 1. You can clarify and agree roles, responsibilities, boundaries, standards, behaviours and what you can expect from each other.

Agree how you will support your team members to develop and achieve their goals, including team tasks and career or lifetime aspirations. Encourage them to be leaders and invest in developing them.

5. Earn the right to lead

How much do your people see you as a leader? How credible and competent are you in their eyes? It is worth stepping into their shoes to view yourself from their perspective. How do your attitude and behaviours as their leader inspire and engage them? What demotivates them? What works well and what do you want to change and improve?

How are you spending your time? Are you focusing on the right things now you are a leader? Or are you still trying to do your last role and not investing enough effort on strategy and this role? Many people find it hard to transition from being the expert, where you value the actual work you do (for example the musician in the orchestra mentioned earlier), to being the leader of experts (for example the conductor). You no longer directly do the work you used to do and value (play music). You now indirectly raise team performance to deliver results, through working with each person to raise their game in how they deliver the work, not just as an individual but working in harmony as a team (play an exquisite orchestral overture). If you find yourself in this transition stage, you could get a lot of benefit working with a coach to change how you value your contribution in work, from the outputs you deliver through your expertise to the more indirect outputs you deliver through developing others.

> ### Case study: From a manager 'David' who I coached through the transition
>
> 'I've been appointed for my expertise and ability and it's my duty to help my reports with that. They come to me with so many requests and problems which I have to sort out. My door is always open; I want to be accessible. Some days feel like I spend the whole time firefighting and there is no time for my strategic role.
>
> 'For example, "Chan" comes to me about problems which I can do with my eyes closed. He has so much on his plate and I can best support him by doing it which gives him time for everything else he is still learning to do. But now I'm working overtime to do my real role. It's impacting on my personal life.'
>
> David recognised that he was reverting to his comfort zone and 'getting my sleeves rolled up and doing what I did before. I recognise I need to let go of that but I don't have time to train him how to do it properly.' We reframed perspectives on help and time. By taking over, David prevented Chan's ability to develop. At first it takes longer to train Chan how to do the things that David could do in a fraction of the time. However, once Chan can do it himself and clear boundaries

have been agreed about when to do it versus when to check first, time is freed up to focus on strategy. Recognise the pull of the comfort zone before leaping blindly back into what you can do effortlessly (habitual thinking; see Chapter 8) and makes you feel good (rewards mastery; Chapter 10).

Case study: How it feels from the level below

'Anika', a manager I coached, felt her confidence had been completely eroded, was demotivated and having difficulty getting respect from her direct reports. She was previously responsible for everything in her role, but in a recent company restructure was given a senior manager. 'Jayne' now wanted to be heavily involved and control decisions, which was severely affecting Anika's need for autonomy and making her feel her role had been demoted. To make matters worse, Jayne was stepping into the classic case of 'doing it for her' when Anika went to talk through decisions, or jumping in to change things when Anika did it differently to how Jayne would have done it. Jayne was communicating directly to Anika's reports, not always giving Anika information required to answer her reports' questions when they came to her about it, which contributed to Anika feeling undermined. Jayne had previously done Anika's role in a different department, had a strong desire to help and was reverting to her comfort zone and continuing to work in the way she had in that role.

Are you creating the environment where people can excel? Find out what your people need from you and from the organisation. How can you shape the organisation's systems and culture to create positive emotions and experiences that foster trust, wellbeing and higher performance? How well do you provide required resources and remove obstacles for them to do their job well? How often are you their obstacle? How do your people perceive the support you are giving them? Your intention is probably to be helpful, share your expertise (which, after all, is why you are in this role) and help them deliver the desired outcomes. Do they receive it as great guidance? Or do they think it is too directive, micromanaging and showing lack of trust? Or something else?

Coaching, 360 degree feedback and using tools such as the Johari window or Perceptual Positions from Neuro Linguistic Programming (NLP) are excellent resources to learn about the alignment or mismatch between how you perceive yourself as a leader and how others perceive you; and between your intentions in how you lead and how others receive it.

Build your confidence and leadership presence, which will make you more credible and inspire other people to have confidence in you. Confidence in yourself makes it easier to learn to trust in others, so that you can step back and distribute leadership through your organisation. Confidence is essential to be able to share responsibility, and give others the autonomy to do their job well, feel confident to ask for support when needed, contribute new ideas, and constantly think about 'the way we work here' and how they could improve processes.

6. Engage each person as an individual – make it personal

Being genuinely interested in knowing each person in your team transforms engagement. It is not so easy to know each individual personally in the wider organisation, so think about how you can interact with them in a way to make them feel recognised. How will they relate to you? How will they see you 'walking the talk'? I once coached a managing director of a busy airport who took the time and effort to get to know staff at all levels in order to be able to greet them by name and stop a few minutes for a conversation, any time he walked through the airport buildings. He made people feel valued and you could see their respect for him as a result.

7. Communicate in ways that engage

First listen to understand (Chapter 4) and when you do speak, tune into the type of communication that resonates with the person (Chapter 5) and have a range of different message delivery styles up your sleeve. Plan what stories you can tell that inspire, engage and get the message across much more vividly and memorably than dry facts alone.

8. Adjust your leadership style and strategy to what the person needs from you at this moment

As leadership is context and relationship dependent, the better you are able to match your style with what a person needs in that situation, the more effective you will be as a leader. Everyone has a preferred or default style, which may or may not be consciously chosen or particularly effective. You tend to default to the leadership styles you have been conditioned to expect from others, as you grew up and in your organisation. Becoming aware of your style opens possibilities for you to be flexible and choose an appropriate style for the situation.

There are many leadership models that can guide you on choosing how to behave. These two are intuitive and cover most situations.

- Situational Leadership (Hersey and Blanchard, 1977; updated by Blanchard and colleagues (1985) to Situational Leadership II), which is about matching your leadership style with the maturity level of the person/team/situation. There are many resources on the Internet that explain it well.

- The Integrated Leadership Model ILM72 (Strycharczyk et al., 2015) integrates components common to many leadership models on six double-ended scales representing different aspects of leadership style. The higher order scales relate to your focus on delivering results and engagement with teams and individuals.

    The ILM72 questionnaire provides your personal profile and enables you to understand your default style, with suggestions for how and when to flex your style. Interestingly, your default style may simply reflect the dominant situation in your work and the prevailing management style. Organisations can find the ILM72 a very useful diagnostic to evaluate leadership effectiveness across the organisation and within different departments (Strycharczyk and Elvin, 2014).

9. Recognise and acknowledge each person in a way that is meaningful for them, and celebrate as a team

Celebrate progress frequently to maintain engagement. Learn what gestures are meaningful for each person when you want to recognise or acknowledge them. Pay and bonuses are good up to a point, but (smaller) personalised gestures that tap into internal motivators (Chapter 10) are more engaging. Many people fall into the trap of taking planned progress for granted, which leaves people feeling undervalued and demotivated.

Tap into shared interests to socialise informally, which builds trust and stronger relationships. For example, some companies have clubs for activities such as sports, book reading, social events or volunteering, or internal work-related networks.

10. Continuous improvement

Don't just react to problems when they occur but be proactive and come up with improvement ideas. Take a good look at where you are now, for yourself and for your organisation/department/team and analyse it in granular detail to understand what is and isn't working or is and isn't aligned with the organisation's purpose and values.

Take time to reflect on why you do things the way you do and question whether there could be a better, more efficient or more effective way. Think of the British Olympic Cycling Team who constantly look at ways to shave off a few fractions of a second here and there; these all add up to the difference between a gold medal and no medals.

Think how you can improve and develop as a person and a leader. Your thoughts and actions now prepare you with the mindset and skills to be in the right place at the right time for future opportunities that will take you on your journey to achieve your lifetime dreams and aspirations. Step out of your comfort zone; expand it by spending more time in your stretch zone. Experiment with things that haven't been done before. Learn to be comfortable taking appropriate risks, starting small and using reflection to learn from your experience, including mistakes and successes.

Sue's brief framework to engage your team

- Know yourself and each person.
- Inspire them with *Why* and *What*.
- Trust them with *How* they will do it (using a coaching style to boost your confidence to step back).
- Provide support and remove obstacles.
- Regularly recognise progress together.
- Evaluate implications for the bigger picture, review and revise.

3. Meaning – purpose, values, vision

The single most important factor for engagement, motivation and job satisfaction is having a sense of meaning and purpose, as consistently revealed by a range of in-depth studies such as those by Thomas (2009) and PwC (2015). Meaning and purpose help a person feel their work matters and collectively brings people together to work in the same direction, making the overall team/organisation more effective in delivering the outcome.

Indeed, having a sense of meaning and purpose can literally make the difference between life and death. Viktor Frankl was an Austrian psychologist who survived the Holocaust and helped other inmates in concentration camps during the First World War. He noticed that survivors of these terrible places were those people who felt a sense of purpose, such as love for their family, a talent they could use or important memories that gave them a meaning to cling to. The people who felt they had nothing to live for died quickest. The people who felt a sense of purpose and meaning were able to choose their attitude, even in the miserable conditions, and survive.

Case study: Purpose

Tom's boss said his global team was one of the most engaged and productive he'd ever come across, despite

> working remotely across different continents and cultures. Tom insists that aligning with purpose was the single most important thing to engage everyone. Many teams might do this at an annual strategy meeting. Tom's team started every single meeting, including the rapid half-hour, weekly team catch-ups, with a reminder of why they were there. Every team member reported activity done, immediate plans and contribution to progress in delivering the purpose. This not only aligns activities to be more effective, with less conflicts and repetition, but also bonds together a diverse group across different time zones, cultures, backgrounds and divergent perspectives and norms (of behaviours and expectations). Team members really care about how their actions impact on others and the common purpose.

Vision and mission

The vision and mission statements are how you translate your purpose into media (words, pictures, video, music, etc.). The mission states in one or two sentences why the organisation exists: what it does, who it does it for and how it does what it does. A compelling vision that defines the desired long-term future for what the organisation will achieve is three times more important than other factors for driving engagement, according to the large global survey by PwC (2015). The more vivid and emotionally connected the vision is, the more it means something to everyone and inspires people to believe in and commit to it. Having an inspiring vision that you are contributing towards helps people believe their work is worthwhile, feel good about what they do and believe in the company they work for.

Share a compelling vision about why your company is here and the direction it is going, to give people confidence in your company. Capturing your vision in a short pithy mantra helps people connect with it day in, day out. For example, Virgin Money's vision is 'Everybody better off' or EBO. Everyone working there can tell you about it and they use EBO to help make daily decisions, from the staff serving at the Virgin Money lounges to senior banking staff.

However, it is not enough to have a great vision, you also need to have aligned goals that everyone can get behind and know how their contribution makes the difference. Co-create a team vision, articulating how it aligns with the organisation's vision. While it takes courage to step back after giving initial direction, encouraging your team to make it their own makes it more meaningful. Identify how each person's role contributes to it, tie daily activity to it, and regularly recognise progress towards it to create consistency and higher productivity as everyone pulls in the same direction.

Case study: Vision

The management team of an events venue spent several days clarifying their vision and values about what they stood for and who were the clients they wanted to attract. In the end they decided on the word 'Magnificent' for their mantra. When defining success they asked, 'What does magnificent mean for us? What is magnificent performance? Who are magnificent clients?' When deciding on how they should work together, they asked, 'How does this make us magnificent? What behaviour leads to magnificent results?' When planning their refurbishment, every decision was passed through the filter, 'What do people expect in a magnificent venue? How will this look magnificent? How will it feel magnificent? How will it sound magnificent?' You get the idea! The outcome transformed the appearance, performance and client satisfaction for the venue as well as staff pride in working there.

3. Meaning – purpose, values, vision

Core values

Values are the things that are most important to you and contribute to how you perceive meaning. Many people are not aware of their values, yet they are the core principles that frequently control decision making at a deep, non-conscious level.

You absorb your values throughout life (see Chapter 8) and values can change as you mature. For example, parents often say how their priorities completely change as soon as they have children and their values shift towards providing stability and protection in order to nurture their family. It is extremely valuable to reflect on what your core values are and examine how constructive they are now for you and your aspirations.

Working in harmony with your values raises your energy levels, motivation, emotional commitment and performance and makes you more authentic. When your core values are conflicted, you feel resistance and stress, both of which lead to negative emotional states, reduced cognitive ability, poor relationships and lower performance (see Chapter 9). Conflicts could happen if you hold two core values that conflict with each other or if you experience a situation or expectation that conflicts with your personal values.

Identify strong organisational core values that have meaning for people inside and outside the organisation (e.g. customers). They show what the company stands for and are the guiding principles for company integrity and consistent decision making throughout the organisation. Identify behaviours associated with each value so people can translate them into everyday activity. Find some alignment or common ground between your personal values, team values and organisational values (see Chapter 2, step 3).

4. Listen – *really* listen to understand

Create a climate where truth is heard and people are comfortable speaking up. Encourage people to contribute ideas, improve processes, air disagreements, constructively examine all perspectives and ultimately commit to action that aligns with the common purpose.

Most people listen in order to follow up with their view and opinion, whether to agree or disagree with the speaker, give their perspective or contribute new ideas. Many managers have conversations like this, with a positive intention of helping the other person, and believe that they are listening. Few people listen with a deep intent to understand from the speaker's perspective, in a way that makes the other person feel valued, heard and understood. Actively listening to understand is an advanced skill that transforms how well you can engage your people. It involves more than just hearing the words. Instead, it includes noticing verbal and non-verbal signals, such as tone of voice, expressions and body language, and actively interacting with the speaker. However, rather than responding with your perspective, your interactions should involve asking questions to clarify meaning and rephrasing and reflecting back their words to show the speaker that you respect and want to understand him or her.

4. Listen – *really* listen to understand

Case study: Working on listening skills

In an event I ran for senior leaders in the public sector, we had group sessions with one-to-one conversations to explore their major challenges. In the first session, the person taking the role of manager/coach genuinely thought they were listening, and were contributing their ideas and experience to support the person to explore their challenge. It was a dialogue like a 'normal' conversation. In the second session, the person in the manager/coach role was asked to explore the other person's challenge using only some combination of the specific listening skills listed on pages 32 and 33. In the group reflection, the leaders noticed that in the second session they got a much better understanding of the challenge, deeper into the challenge more quickly, and the person with the challenge felt the other person had shown more interest and understood them better.

Case study: Listening to empower

One of my one-to-one coaching clients, 'Jen', took on a manager's role in an organisation that was traditionally very hierarchical and authoritarian. When people on her team came to her with questions about what to do, she would ask, 'How are you doing it now?' and follow up with, 'How can you do it better?' Then she would explore with them why they think that would work, what the potential barriers might be, how they could recognise whether it is going as expected and suggest the person try out their idea. At first she found resistance from some people, who were used to getting direction. However, other team members loved it, saying they think Jen respects their opinion and they feel heard. Jen believes this approach builds trust and empowers her people, as it confirms to them that they can come up with their own solution and their ideas do work, which they are more engaged with implementing.

Listening in meetings

In a group setting, create a climate of open curiosity where all ideas can be contributed and further information elicited without judgement. In meetings, it is often difficult for people to feel heard when they have questions about an item on the agenda, as there is usually a tight schedule and the meeting chairperson has the positive intention of not letting the meeting drag on over the time allotted and make people late for their next commitment. These situations can be highly detrimental to engagement when people feel their concerns are not being heard.

Case study: Over to you

One of my coaching clients, 'Akiko', was brought in at the last minute to lead a team very behind schedule and the project deadline within two weeks. They had not been told about the replacement and were very hostile. Meetings erupted and overran as people didn't listen to updates and heckled. In our session, Akiko identified that people felt their concerns were not being heard, and there wasn't enough time for more than a few questions at the end of presentations. She added a specific item to the agenda called 'Over to you' to listen to audience concerns, and committed to give or find answers. Overtly having listening on the agenda, plus walking around the buildings to connect with people individually, transformed hostility to engagement within a week. The team became determined and committed to deliver the project on time.

Active listening skills

Show you are paying attention, which raises confidence and trust

- Be curious, interested and non-judgemental; find something interesting in what the speaker is saying.
- Create a good environment for a meeting; consider the room layout and your relative positions.
- Create rapport, for example maintain a healthy eye contact.
- Keep opinions, assumptions and advice to yourself until the appropriate time to share them (which may not arise – e.g. in a coaching conversation).

Notice the non-verbal signals and emotional undertones

These include intensity, tone of voice, emphasis, hesitations, speed at which they speak and other non-verbal signals. How well do they align with what the person is saying?

Listen to the content and interact in ways seeking to understand

- *Encourage*: you can use body language, actions, noises and words (e.g. hmm, oh, carry on, yes?) to encourage the speaker to continue without breaking their flow of thoughts.
- *Open questions*: most people tend to ask questions that are directed by their own train of thought and assumptions, or are closed (yes/no answer). Be aware and ask open questions (e.g. starting with the 6Ws – what, where, how, why, when, who, though take care with using 'why' as it can come across as judgemental or blaming). Clean language questions, developed by David Grove, are an extreme form of open questions working with metaphor and the person's

words. From NLP, another useful and very powerful question is 'What would be the most useful question for me to ask you just now?' It is surprising how someone who feels stuck is able to answer this when you give them time (and silence) for it to emerge, and discover a way to become unstuck.

- *Clarify*: ask questions to reduce ambiguity and establish clarity.
- *Elaborate and probe*: ask questions more concerned with delving deeper into the topic and the person's thoughts, beliefs, interpretations, motivations and feelings, to lead to greater insights.
- *Reflect*: repeat back to the person their key words and phrases. Hearing your own words spoken out loud by someone else makes you feel better understood and can remarkably clarify your thoughts and awareness of your emotional state.
- *Paraphrase*: interpret in your own words what the other person says to check whether you've understood what was intended. If you have a different understanding, paraphrasing can break the flow but leads to insights for both of you, especially if that misunderstanding is at the root of an issue.
- *Integrate and summarise*: succinctly outline the topic discussed and check for clarity, understanding and agreement. This is a particularly useful skill to develop as not everyone has the oversight to pull various threads of discussion together. It transforms outcomes from meetings, yet often appears to be lacking (even in board meetings).

Potential barriers to listening and understanding

- *Time pressures*: short meeting times, long agendas and so on influence people to control the direction of the conversation and make it hard to listen to dialogue, especially when it might seem off topic, or allow thinking time. Similarly, allowing time to check for group level understanding of what the speaker intended to convey can feel like a waste of time – everyone assumes their interpretation is correct, which can lead to misunderstandings of what has or hasn't been agreed.

- *Preoccupation*: personal concerns or multitasking (e.g. checking email/the web/other notes, etc. while in a meeting) prevents you from listening properly.

- *Defensiveness*: if either person feels threatened by what is said, the real message is not heard as information is distorted or blocked out. Raising awareness to recognise when either of you is being defensive, gives you a chance to explore why. Reflect with compassion and gently uncover what is happening.

- *Talking too much*: many people talk too much, too soon, especially when they like to share ideas, information and experience and want to help the other person. Interruptions and questions can disrupt the person's flow and confidence. Controlling the direction of the conversation can lead to undesired outcomes. For example, if you only explore your perspective on an issue, you don't discover the perspectives of others in the room, which can result in creating strategies that don't address the real problems and fail to make improvements. Active listening to all perspectives generates a more accurate analysis of the issue, the result of which is more likely to be successful actions for improvements.

- *Fear of silence*: many people feel uncomfortable with silence. Silence often seems like a waste of time, when nothing is happening or no progress is being made, yet silent time for reflection or thinking is usually the key for gaining insight.

- *Diversity*: different personalities, working styles, frames of reference, backgrounds, cultures and languages can make listening to understand more demanding and frustrating on both sides. Diversity brings great benefits for performance when you create a culture to embrace different perspectives and make time to clarify and elaborate where necessary in order to understand the words and check whether your interpretation matches their intended meaning and message.

"

Communicating with influence is about small things we do that affect the environment and people around us.

Joe Navarro

"

5. Communicate

Sadly, facts don't usually speak for themselves (as much as many people feel that they should). It is how the messenger puts them across that determines how the facts are understood and their significance interpreted. A confident messenger who understands your interests is more credible and convincing.

Body language

Your inner thoughts and feelings leak out through your tone of voice and body language, which is read by others unconsciously and perceived as intuition or gut feel. According to Joe Navarro (2009), an FBI specialist on body language, when there is a mismatch to words, body language is prioritised as the most honest and trustworthy communication. You need to ensure all three are aligned and consistent to have a believable message.

- Build rapport through body language and the environment you create around yourself, so you feel comfortable and connected with each other. Navarro suggests that you consider your position relative to each other (half-facing at 90 degrees is less confrontational than fully face on) and appropriate eye contact (too much is creepy; not enough can be interpreted that you are hiding something).

- Reinforce points as you speak using gestures that are authentic to you. Copying someone else's gestures is less credible.

- Be aware of your tone of voice and notice the message conveyed. A hesitant tone reduces other people's confidence in what you are saying. It comes across as though you don't believe it, in which case why should they believe it. When you believe in what you say, but you lack confidence, practise saying it out loud in a strong calm tone of voice and with a confident posture so it becomes more familiar.

- Confidence shows in an open, straight posture with head high, good eye contact, positive gestures such as smiling and a calm, strong tone of voice. Confidence depends not only on your actual ability or competence, but also on how you assess your ability. You can raise your confidence through preparing in advance, knowing your content is correct and accurate and holding a positive mindset.

Sensory language

Most people have a dominant sense that is reflected in their language. Matching your communication to their sensory preference builds a stronger sense of connection more quickly (for a good guide, see Knight, 2009). Use all senses to make your message resonate with a wider audience. Table 1 provides a few examples of sensory words and phrases.

Table 1: Sensory words

Visual	Clarity, focus, horizon, outlook, view
Auditory	Articulate, communicate, harmony, hidden message, ring bells

Kinaesthetic	Go with the flow, gut feeling, handle, intuition, stress
Taste/smell	Bite-size, bland, in essence, spice it up, zest
General or non-sensory	Accomplish, create, deliver, manage, understand

Match communication channels

You engage a person's interest far better when you communicate in a channel that holds meaning for them so they can get the significance of what you are saying.

Engineers, scientists, accountants and many other technical professions are trained to primarily communicate facts. However, when the person you need to influence or persuade doesn't value facts to the same extent you do, or doesn't have time or knowledge to interpret the significance of the facts, you need to communicate more than just the facts.

Case study: Communicating your contribution

One of my clients, 'Indira', had been turned down for promotion and said to me, 'I don't understand. My boss says that the quality of my work is higher than my colleague's yet he is putting my colleague forward for promotion. It's not fair, you should be promoted on merit not on politicking and how you talk up your work.' However, on examination, we discovered that Indira told her boss what she had done and the results delivered, and expected the facts should speak for themselves. In effect, she was assuming that because her boss appreciated the quality of results he also noticed the significance to the business – how they aligned with core

> strategy and contributed towards achieving priority goals. But her boss was busy with his own role and managing other managers, so probably didn't have time to interpret their significance. The double benefit of speaking about results delivered and the meaning and contribution to progress is that her boss would understand the significance and additionally see her potential for promotion because she was demonstrating strategic thinking.

Shell and Moussa (2008) describe how it is important to craft your message to flow through different communication channels, particularly when you want to persuade someone to believe in your ideas. Some examples:

- Rational thought and practical reason – facts and evidence: ensure accuracy, no bias (i.e. you have all the evidence) and that data are referenced for credibility. However, people interpret evidence through the filter of their mindset and perspectives, so there needs to be more.

- Paint pictures with words: metaphors and stories are memorable due to the way memory is structured in the brain to connect different items together and because they elicit emotion when people relate to them. Use stories to help people to connect with your message and see how it relates to them personally or to issues they know and/or care about. It leads to better understanding than just plain facts.

- Inspiration and emotion – vision, purpose, spiritual, tap into motivators: invite people to share in the vision, share values, beliefs and experiences. Identify how your message or idea is significant and strategically aligns with the common purpose. Consider how your words can be energising and motivating.

- Negotiating: I will do x if you do y.

- Ask for help and invite commitment.
- Consider whether you need to work through alliances to get your message heard.
- Build positive relationships through building rapport, and highlight areas of similarity, liking and reciprocity in your message to enhance the chance of it being heard.
- Big picture versus detail: many senior executives have a preference for big picture/strategic thinking, and if you don't start your message here, they can't listen to the details.

Prepare your content

- Clarify your objective.
- Know your audience: research (including listening first) their interests, expectations and preferred communication channels.
- Structure your message:
    - start with why it is relevant (purpose, big picture)
    - what: the main message
    - how does it work? What must you explain and what can you ask?
    - implications: what happens if you do or don't do this? How does it impact strategic goals?

> The person born with a talent they are meant to use will find their greatest happiness in using it.
>
> **Johann Wolfgang von Goethe**

6. Working to strengths

Strengths are inner capabilities and resources, your unique combination of talents, knowledge and skills that energise and enable you to perform at your best. Many people don't know their strengths and talents; they're the things you find so easy and so simple that you take them for granted and assume 'anyone could do it'. In fact, 'anyone' can't. You can, and other people would find it invaluable for you to do it for them or with them. Learn to celebrate your strengths.

What you are good at is not necessarily a strength. Your strengths are the things that come naturally to you, that you enjoy doing, that bring you energy. Anything that you are good at but drains your energy, or is not something you would choose to do, is just something you do well (so it's good to recognise that) but it is not a core strength.

Why are strengths important?

- Recognising and applying strengths in work raises job satisfaction, fulfilment, commitment and engagement, which leads to the benefits Gallup (2013) and others have identified such as staff retention, customer satisfaction, productivity and profitability for the organisation.

6. Working to strengths

- Top performing managers focus on strengths. They help people to discover their strengths and set strengths-based goals, spend time with high performers, match strengths with projects and emphasise strengths over seniority when assigning roles.

- Knowing what you are good at and using your strengths to be part of something you believe in gives you a more meaningful life and is associated with higher happiness and optimism.

- You don't need to be the best before you can believe you are good at something! Recognising and acknowledging what you are good at and providing evidence to reassure yourself that you are not making false claims, raises self-belief, esteem, confidence and capability.

- Know your edge and the value you bring to the organisation. Be able to articulate your strengths and competence as that inspires belief and confidence in you by other people. As a leader, this helps people working with you feel more engaged.

Build on strengths and manage around weaknesses

Building on strengths is far more productive than eliminating weaknesses. When you work to strengths you are 'in the zone' or 'in flow' and feel positive emotions that enhance your capacity for using your cognitive brain and raising performance. Acknowledge and manage weaknesses; don't ignore them. Build confidence by recognising that you can't be good at everything, especially things that drain your energy and motivation. Recognising your limitations gives you the opportunity to manage work and life so you do not have to do things that drain you, but instead can work to strengths as much as possible.

Strengths and weaknesses are a balancing act. Weaknesses are qualities/strengths that are out of balance in that context.

Consider what positive attributes are associated with your weaknesses and how you respond in different situations. For example, flexibility is a strength. If you overdo it, you become aimless, which is a weakness. If you underdo flexibility, you can become rigid in your thinking and no longer open to new ideas, which can also be a weakness. Other examples: respectful of others becomes disrespectful when underdone or deferential when overdone. Confidence underdone becomes timorous, while overdone is arrogant.

Review your strengths and consider whether there are situations when you overdo them, or are perceived by others to overdo them. For example: assertiveness underdone is passive and overdone becomes aggressive. People who have high mental toughness may believe they are acting assertively, and are perceived as being assertive by colleagues who also have high mental toughness, but can be perceived as being aggressive by colleagues who are mentally sensitive.

Strengths assessments

Doing an assessment helps you notice the strengths you are taking for granted. For example, one of my clients who completed the VIA Inventory of Strengths said,

> Surprisingly, my top strength turned out to be judgement. I thought that was bad at first, but then discovered that it means critical thinking. Thinking things through and examining them from all sides; not jumping to conclusions; being able to change one's mind in light of evidence; weighing all evidence fairly. And when I thought about it, I realised that I've always been good at seeing different perspectives, researching evidence and writing essays and reports that clearly present both (or more) sides of the argument, even those I don't agree with.

6. Working to strengths

There are several strengths assessments available on the internet to discover generic strengths. Two of the best are:

- VIA Inventory of Strengths derived from positive psychology research led by Martin Seligman. It gives your ranking in 24 character strengths relevant to life and work. The basic report is free (viacharacter.org).
- *Strengthsfinder 2.0* by Tom Rath. It gives your top five work strengths based on Gallup research. The book includes a code for the online questionnaire and describes all strengths, how to use each when it is yours and how to work with someone who has this strength.

Discovering your strengths – what is going right (rather than wrong) for you?

Use these questions to start to uncover your personal strengths.

- What are you are proud of?
- What do you love doing? What makes you feel energised, fulfilled, happy, optimistic, content or other feelings of wellbeing?
- What do you excel at, sometimes without really trying?
- How would you spend your time if you could do anything?
- What do other people say you are good at?
- List your strengths. Be specific. Where are they on the underdone–strength–overdone scale in different contexts?

Using your strengths in work:

- What strengths do you currently bring to your work? What would you like to use more?
- How could you bring strengths you enjoy elsewhere into work? What difference would that make?

- What strengths are you overdoing, to the extent that they have now become a weakness to you in work – in some or all situations? What do you want to do about that?
- Build personal development plans around enhancing strengths. The results are better for wellbeing, performance, productivity and ultimately profitability.

Team building

Build your team around recognising strengths and matching roles to strengths. Identifying strengths as a team raises awareness of diversity within the group, ability to appreciate different perspectives and a common language that helps you to harness the benefits of diversity when working together.

1. For each person, put a photo with a large piece of paper below it on the wall and ask all team members to write about the strengths they see in that team member. Include what you admire about them: positive qualities, capabilities, skills, attitudes and achievements. Every time I do this exercise with client teams, it is fascinating how many members say they are amazed, as no one has said this about them before.

2. Each team member shares their top five strengths from a profile like *Strengthsfinder* and talks about examples of how they use it in work and outside work. It stimulates thinking about how you can draw on each team member for different parts of a project and work to strengths together. It also helps to create strong team relationships as members get to know and like each other more.

At one organisation I work with, people put their top five strengths on their name plate above their computer at hot-desks. It maintains a culture of actively working to strengths and promotes people recognising each other positively.

> Coaching is unlocking a person's potential to maximise their own performance. It is about raising awareness and reducing interference.
>
> **W. Timothy Gallwey**
> *The Inner Game of Work*

7. Coaching

Coaching is a process that raises awareness, clarity and focus; encourages people to take on responsibility; and reduces barriers to performance.

Many managers believe they are using a coaching approach but actually still hold responsibility themselves rather than allowing the other person to be responsible as much as possible – for example for jointly identifying desired outcomes, for choosing the appropriate methodology that will be most effective and efficient given their personal resources (mental toughness, emotional intelligence, attitudes, confidence, working style, capabilities, knowledge, expertise, etc.) and the available external resources (e.g. organisational procedures/systems, equipment, finance, other people, etc.).

I highly recommend attending at least a basic course in coaching skills, if you have not already done so, when you truly want to engage your people. Coaching is a practical skill best learned with demonstration and practise, not from a book.

A few tenets of coaching

- Coaching at its simplest is a conversation that follows a process or framework that allows the coachee (person receiving coaching) to gain new insights, arrive at their own

7. Coaching

conclusions, and choose their commitments. The difficulty for many managers is to coach without imposing their own agenda, thoughts, opinions and so on.

- Coaching may happen during informal conversations, from 5 minutes or more, to formal sessions, typically lasting 30 minutes to 2 hours.

- Responsibility lies with the coachee.

- The coach provides the process while the coachee provides the content.

- Listening and questioning are vital tools (Chapter 4). Typically, a coachee will speak about 70 per cent or more of the time.

- Coaching is future focused and a process to set goals in a changing context, raise awareness, clarify where to focus attention, and commit to action within specified time frames with accountability.

- Coaching raises the quality of work and learning, and optimises managers' use of time in the long term (although not the immediate short term when new learning is required).

- As Whitmore describes in *Coaching for Performance* (2002), by responding to questions, the coachee understands the context, potential options that are viable or not viable, what is required to achieve the goal, and takes responsibility for the chosen actions. At the same time, the manager understands the thinking that underlies the action plan and the waypoints to recognise success or departure from the plan, which gives them more confidence to step back. This gives the manager more time to focus on aspects of their role that only they can do. Paradoxically, this gives the manager more 'control', especially as the coachee is more likely to undertake the actions committed to, even when the manager is not around, than if the manager had told them exactly what to do, and how and when to do it.

- Coaching is a process that raises accountability for your goals. Research has shown that people who talk about specific aspirations and commit to them publicly are more successful in achieving them. Committing in advance to a review and accountability appointment raises success even more.

Process – T-GROW

The framework for a coaching conversation is a process that guides your approach and is invisible to the coachee as they are focused on their content. There are many effective coaching processes. GROW, described by Whitmore (2002), is one process that works well for leaders and managers wanting to engage people, and we add T to it as most people start with a topic rather than a coachable goal.

T Topic – a coachee usually presents their goal as a topic too large to address in a coaching session.

G Goal – focuses on refining and uncovering the real goal for the session.

R Reality – explores the coachee's perspective of the situation and challenges them to think of alternative perspectives. Sometimes the session goal needs to be revisited and redefined.

O Options – the coachee thinks of a wide range of potential ways to achieve their goal and identifies which steps (if any) may need to be sequential. Conversations may cycle between Options and Reality.

W Will – the coach supports the client to evaluate and choose options and commit to them.

7. Coaching

Goal Setting

Many managers set work goals for their people. A coaching approach encourages you to support your people to set their own goals, tapping into their own motivations, which results in greater ownership and engagement. No matter what process you use, always ensure that goals are aligned with the common purpose to keep your team pulling together more effectively.

Poorly designed goals can be demotivating. The reason many goals fail is because they only include an outcome that is not 100 per cent directly within your control and/or that the gap between where you are now and the outcome seems too big to be possible.

To successfully set and achieve goals

1. Write down your purpose (personal/team/organisation vision, your *Why*; Chapter 3).

2. Identify the outcome you want to achieve – your intention, the *What* – and check that it aligns with your purpose. Capture this with a short, pithy mantra to foster focus and momentum.

3. Create process goals that are *How* you will do it. These are actions within your direct control.

4. Break down the process goals into short actionable single item steps.

5. Put the steps in sequence to plan your route map to achieve your goal. Start with quick, easy steps that instantly show progress. If you don't have any, you haven't broken down your steps to be small enough.

6. Explore the implications and potential intended and unintended outcomes. How does it contribute progress to the *Why*? What needs to be adjusted?

7. Identify barriers and the hidden benefit of the status quo. For example, your goal to stop smoking will mean you lose regular five minute conversations with the director two levels above you during smoking breaks. This informal mentoring relationship holds enormous benefit for you. How can you retain this hidden benefit while doing what it takes to achieve your goal?

8. Schedule the steps and commit to do them.

9. Visualise or mentally rehearse how you do it and what waypoints and outcomes look and feel like, to improve motivation and successful achievement.

10. Remember to celebrate achieving steps – even small, personal celebrations for small steps help you to revitalise, recognise progress and maintain motivation for the ultimate goal. Studies show that sharing progress publicly (e.g. in the office, on Twitter, etc.) helps you to achieve your goals better and faster.

Most managers are familiar with SMART goals yet there are some additional aspects to consider to co-create truly engaging goals with your coachee (and for your own goals). Set SMARTER REAP goals:

- *S*pecific
- *M*easurable
- *A*greed and understood
- *R*ealistic
- *T*ime framed

- *E*xciting: challenging, stretching, energising, motivating and inspiring
- *R*eview and revise – be accountable and respond to changing circumstances and opportunities

- *R*elevant: purposeful and appropriate
- *E*thical and environmentally sound
- *A*ligned and congruent with your personal and organisational values
- *P*resent tense. *P*ositively stated. *P*ersonal. *P*ossible. Set goals for what you do want.

The 4Ps of REAP are most often left out of goals at work, yet these are critical to raise ownership and motivation. Download a detailed version from my online resources.

8. Understanding mindset

Mindset determines success

Did you know that senior business executives attribute about 80 per cent of their performance to mindset, while professional and elite athletes attribute 90–95 per cent of their success to their mindset? Even though we imagine that when athletes compete, it is their sport skills that are most important, the athletes themselves say the most important part of their success is their mindset. For example, in 2012, before the London Olympics, Mo Farah talked about how he used to want to win but in some part of his mind he would think his competitors were better than him and he would lose the race when they came up alongside him. Now he's worked on his mindset, confidence and his inner knowledge that he can beat them, he's no longer focusing on the other competitors, he is focused on winning. (And succeeding – with gold medals at the 2012 and 2016 Olympics, World and European Championships.) He feels that confidence is like a weapon that gives you control, and you feel positive knowing you've prepared well. In contrast, self-doubt clouds your mind with excessive negative thoughts about the outcome, not being good enough and so on. When you come under pressure, this holds you back and you make more errors instead of remaining calm and focused.

8. Understanding mindset

What is mindset?

Your mindset is your frame of reference or perspective for how you interpret the world about you. People often talk about mindset by referring to the outward attributes that reflect our inner overall attitude or mindset. Some of the most important attributes for engaging yourself and other people are a positive attitude, motivation, confidence, emotional intelligence and mental toughness. Other important visible attributes for a high-performance mindset include being purposeful, focused, disciplined and determined.

However, it is your inner attitude or mindset that shapes how you show up in the world and determines your behaviour, actions and outcomes. Your mindset is the filter through which you interpret everything in the world about you (see Chapter 9). The filter includes your beliefs, values, past experiences, sense of identity, self-esteem and so on. Mindset filters are there for a good purpose. Too much noise happens in the world around us to be able to focus and concentrate on it all at once. So the unconscious brain filters out the unimportant noise and sends important information to the conscious, cognitive brain.

Filters help you to focus on what is important and result in your expectation shaping reality: you see what you expect to see and that 'evidence' reinforces your expectations in a self-fulfilling loop, as is described by Chris Argyris (1990) as the 'Ladder of Inference'. This is well demonstrated by the placebo effect: when someone is told they are given a painkiller, they often feel better even if the pill contained no painkiller.

Case study: Filters

When we were looking for a new car, I liked the idea of getting the midnight blue colour and my partner thought that

> would be different, as he'd never seen this model in blue. However, on our way home, we saw lots of them – this model in midnight blue. Suddenly, this was relevant and all visual information that had previously got filtered out now got through. However, his experience of it was that yesterday there were none and today there were lots: what had happened out there to suddenly bring out all the blue models of this car? This is a classic example of how we attribute blocks in our mindset to being external issues. This is why raising awareness of your mindset and your perspective on the world can have far-reaching impacts by removing barriers and raising performance.

Belief

If you want to encourage people to change behaviour and be more engaged, you need to understand both the current behaviour and what mindset underlies it, particularly the beliefs and values. Beliefs are the narratives we tell ourselves to make sense of the world around us. Beliefs underpin our values, which are the principles we believe are most important to uphold in our life (Chapter 3). Our beliefs, especially what we believe is possible or not possible, determine our behaviour and our willingness to try something or put effort into something.

Implications of mindset in the workplace

- When you believe you can do whatever it is you need to, you invest more effort into making it happen. It is important to create a sense of 'it being possible', no matter what setbacks might occur along the way.
- Because your self-perception and beliefs leak out through your body language, people respond and treat you according

to how you see and believe in yourself. You need to believe in yourself as a leader first to grow your leadership presence and for other people to believe in you as a leader. Many managers and executives find one-to-one coaching to grow their leadership mindset is extremely valuable.

- What you believe about a team member makes an enormous impact on their performance. When you expect someone to perform well, your behaviour shows that you trust them and believe they can do the work well, within the time frame and to required standards. You notice what they do well (see Ladder of Inference above – you notice what you are looking for) and acknowledge it. You draw out their best and they perform well. When you expect underperformance, you are likely to notice instances of it and start micromanaging and displaying other behaviours that are demotivating, which engenders poorer performance.

- When you repeatedly demonstrate belief in someone who lacks confidence, give evidence of why they can do it, and support and stretch them to live up to their full potential, you raise their confidence and also help them to engage positively at work. For example, when I worked in a research lab we recruited a technician who had previously worked in a shop and doubted her ability to do lab work. However, she also managed a stable yard with competition horses, so I helped her to recognise that she had the skills to work with animals in the lab even if they were water fleas in jam jars instead of horses in stables: she could manage a schedule for feeding, cleaning and a specialist training regime and she could be reliable and responsible. The specific activities required in the lab were different but the general concept was the same, which is why I believed she would be competent. She knew she was highly competent with horses and once she saw the connection, she believed in herself and became an excellent technician.

- People consistently describe their most inspiring boss as the person who saw something in them that they didn't see themselves; who gave them the confidence and self-belief that transformed their life and career.
- Selective attention focus can have surprising, unintended consequences, such as unconscious bias, which can be costly for an organisation. Gaining multiple perspectives could partly explain why raising diversity raises performance when the team embrace working with difference.

Changing mindset

You learn and evolve your mindset throughout your life, absorbing unconscious conditioning through upbringing, family, culture, education, past experiences, working environment, organisational culture, authority figures, role models and more. These shape your attitude, values, beliefs, sense of purpose, sense of self, how you think about your experiences, your thinking style, focus of attention and so on. Throughout your life you absorb new filters based on what is relevant and important at that time. In time, the world changes, you change, situations change, and what was relevant at one time may no longer apply now. However, most people keep on applying out-of-date filters because they don't know they exist. Yet, because you have learned your mindset, you can also choose to change it and make sure filters 'let through' everything that is relevant to you now. The first step is raising awareness (see Chapter 2, Step 1).

The benefits of becoming aware of your mindset include:

- Revealing the hidden assumptions you make and your unconscious biases.

8. Understanding mindset

- Understanding your perspective and other people's perspectives.
- Noticing more opportunities.
- Discovering possibilities of choice and options. (Even if they are unpalatable, the fact that you have rejected them means your chosen action is intentional and aligned with your values. Recognising this reduces your stress and sense of helplessness or frustration at perceiving you have no choice. See Chapter 10.)
- Choosing your own sense of self and being in control of you (see Chapter 10).

Neuroscience research shows that we can change our mindset. In the past, scientists believed that the brain's neurons were fixed and we lost them as we aged. New imaging techniques enabled scientists to study how live brains work and discover that even adult brains have plasticity (can change shape or structure) and grow new connections (neural pathways) and new brain cells (neurons) when we learn. Making new connections creates 'eureka' moments or sparks of insight. When that thought or connection is used repeatedly, it builds a stronger pathway, much like a footpath appears on a lawn when many people walk across it. The more often a pathway is used, the more the structure becomes ingrained and operates faster in response to the stimulus – more like a motorway than a footpath. When a neural pathway is not used, it gradually starts to break down, though any instance of reuse rebuilds it. This is how we lay down and lose memories and habits.

Habits

Habits reside in the unconscious part of the brain, where you store everything you want to do automatically without having to think them through all the time – such as how to drive a car, the practical skills you use in work or sport, how you prioritise your time, the way you behave in specific situations, your good and bad habits. When you want to change a long-term habitual behaviour, you need to break the automatic stimulation of the fast neural pathway, which means you need first to recognise what triggers that behaviour and deliberately do something that stops the thought and emotions (called breaking state). Changing habitual behaviour takes time and is much harder than learning a new skill.

1. You have to break state because the old habit kicks in first and you have to override it with your chosen behaviour. This is experienced as pain or discomfort, because the brain sends signals that something is wrong when the habitual pathway is not followed (creating the allure of the comfort zone).

2. The habitual neural pathways have to break down through disuse.

3. You build new neural pathways. Learning a new skill just requires this step.

This makes it hard to break habits or change behaviour when you really want to, let alone because someone else tells you to. It compounds the difficulties of changing culture and attitudes throughout the organisation.

Growth mindset

Developing a growth mindset helps you to change habits. Research by Carol Dweck (2012) and other research groups shows that having a growth mindset means you believe you can develop abilities and are open to learning, trying out new ways of doing things and embracing challenges. You can encourage this 'learn and help learn' perspective through praising effort,

8. Understanding mindset

which develops the perspective that success derives from your actions and means you can learn from criticism, persist through setbacks, learn and be inspired by other people's success. It builds your resilience and results in higher levels of success.

In contrast, people with a fixed mindset operate more from a 'judge and be judged' perspective where things are already established and can't be changed. You can inadvertently encourage a fixed mindset by praising ability (e.g. you did well in that test, you must be clever) which leads to connecting outcomes with your identity and a desire to look smart. As a result you avoid challenges or taking risks, as they are threatening opportunities to fail, to get it wrong, to not know what to do and to be shown up. You see effort as a waste of time, give up easily or get defensive at setbacks or criticism, and regard other people's success as evidence of your failure or shortcomings. It reduces your ability to achieve your full potential and reduces your resilience, so you become more stressed through periods of change.

9. The power of positive

Making sense of the outside world

Your body is continuously bombarded by sensory information about the outside world – visual (sight), auditory (sound), kinaesthetic (touch), olfactory (smell) and gustatory (taste) through which you create your own internal representation of the world about you (Figure 2).

To prevent system overload in the cognitive pathway, only 'relevant' information filters through your mindset, influencing your interpretation and decisions. The cognitive pathway is in the neocortex area of the brain, which is important for consciousness, working memory, logic, language, abstract thought, imagination, reasoning, forward planning, complex decision making and learning. It requires energy and is easily fatigued.

All information is processed through the amygdala, which acts as the guardhouse for the emotional pathway or limbic system that is important for unconscious knowledge, emotions, value judgements, memories and habits. The amygdala 'decides' instantly whether the stimuli represent a potential threat or not, assessing among other things the emotional loading and relevance to past experience.

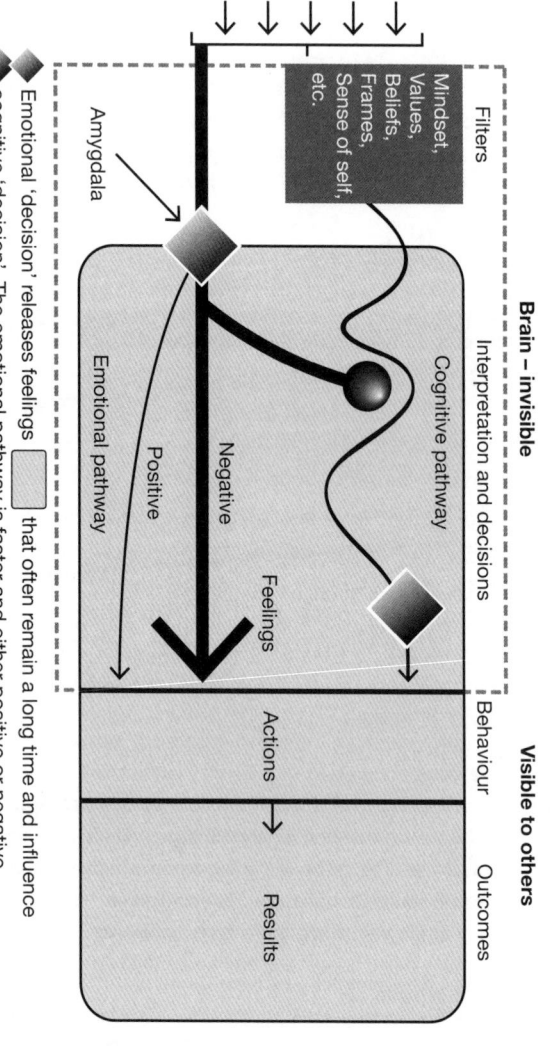

Figure 2 How the brain interprets the outside world and drives behaviour and outcomes

While both pathways operate in fractions of seconds, the cognitive pathway is significantly slower than the emotional pathway, which means that:

- even when we believe we have made a decision based only on rational grounds and evidence, that decision has been shaped both by our mindset determining our frame of reference or perspective and the emotional state in our brain and body
- habitual thinking patterns that require little or no energy kick in before rational thought can override them.

In the 'emotional pathway' the brain is structured to activate either the reward system, which stimulates positive emotions and 'approach behaviours', or the threat system, which stimulates negative emotions and 'avoidance behaviour' (i.e. you can't have both positive and negative emotions at the same time).

Since the consequences of threats can be catastrophic, the negative pathways operate much faster and stronger than the positive neural pathways in the brain, so we can respond immediately we detect any potential threat. Brains have evolved this way as the person who didn't notice the sabre-toothed tiger behind the bushes died and people who had fast reactions to notice potential threats survived. As well as preventing activation in the positive pathway, the negative pathway closes down the cognitive areas of the brain, significantly diminishing capacity for rational thinking, creativity, innovation, problem solving, sparking of ideas and solution finding. Energy is redirected to keep the body safe. The response is the same whether it is a physical threat to safety or a perceived or social threat – such as perceptions of unfairness, or criticism from a manager.

The threat response operates at a very deep, non-conscious, emotional level that most people are unaware of and are unable to override consciously. Sometimes a seemingly innocuous situation triggers a major threat response. You can recognise this amygdala hijack as a strong emotional reaction that happens fast and is inappropriate. Examples are road rage when someone speeds up and drives aggressively close behind you because you overtook them, or responding angrily to a polite request for information.

Mind-body connection

Recent neuroscience research has shown that mind and body are strongly connected with two-way communication between the brain in the head and the mini-brain-like neural systems around the heart and gut, which are also information encoding and processing centres with neuroplasticity. It supports that your thoughts leak out through your body language and substantiates the old adage 'when things go wrong, keep your head up and smile'. When you feel good, the brain's reward centre stimulates neurochemicals that make you smile spontaneously. Conversely, when you don't feel happy, the act of smiling releases the same neurochemicals that make you feel good. The way you act makes you think the same way.

This means that you can change your emotional state by thinking about it and/or by holding your body in the posture associated with the emotional state you want.

Posture and power poses

Amy Cuddy (2012), a professor at Harvard University, showed that holding a 'high-power' pose for only two minutes changes your brain chemistry (raises testosterone and reduces cortisol) and makes you feel more confident, competent and powerful for some time afterwards. Adopting body postures that convey competence and confidence make you feel and think that way and show more enthusiasm, which boosts your performance and ability to cope with stressful situations. Be aware, though, that low-power postures do the opposite, diminishing your ability to inspire and engage other people.

If you are feeling nervous or uncomfortable, the chances are that you will hold a low-power posture, which reinforces a reduction in self-belief, confidence and so on. Just imagine the damage that will do to your performance and other people's belief and trust in you – for example in an interview or a presentation where you want to persuade people to follow your ideas and get engaged. Choose to change to a resourceful, positive state. You can do high-state power poses in private. In public, choose toned-down postures which show confidence and competence more than strength or dominance, such as standing with an open front, shoulders back and head high.

Mirror neurons

Emotions are contagious. Recent research has discovered mirror neurons that fire when we do something and also fire when we see someone else do the same action. For example, if you see someone fall down, you automatically wince as if you had fallen yourself; you automatically smile when someone smiles at you or even if you see people smiling on TV. Mirror neurons are involved in empathy, understanding other people and building better relationships.

Consequences of how the brain works for engaging your people

- The reward system must be activated for people to feel engaged at work, which means the activities, culture, systems, processes and people at work must avoid activating someone's threat system. That is not easy!

9. The power of positive

- It is much easier to trigger negative emotion and responses than positive ones. It can be easy to trigger threat responses unintentionally when someone else interprets your words or actions differently from your intention (Rock, 2008; Chapter 10).

- Our brains are hardwired to focus attention on negative outcomes and things that are different, out of place or unexpected. Additionally, technical professional training and organisational processes compound the effect as they typically focus on detecting what is wrong and problem solving. For example, when I draw a dot on a piece of paper and ask people what they see, most say there is a black spot and ignore that most of it is white space. They take for granted the page that the spot is written on. In the same way, people tend to focus on what they haven't done, immediately notice mistakes and don't notice everything that went well and according to plan.

  To counteract brain hardwiring, training and systematic problem focus:

  o you need to be very intentional about noticing positive outcomes and creating positive experiences

  o it takes about five to seven positive experiences to counteract one negative experience.

- Fear, uncertainty, negative self-talk, doubts, criticism, stress, poor relationships, organisational blame culture, dysfunctional systems and processes, and so on all create threat responses in our brains and diminish our capacity to be our best and perform at our best. It means we can't think rationally or creatively, make good decisions, solve problems, respond well or listen well. Because the negative emotion continues for some time, unless replaced with a positive state, it has a lasting impact on cognitive ability and stimulates avoidance behaviours that can be destructive and perpetuate a negative culture, climate of distrust, destructive relationships and poor performance.

- When you create a positive environment, you stimulate the reward system that puts people in a positive emotional state, which means they:

    o have full access to their cognitive abilities, enabling them to realise their full potential in work, which ultimately leads to higher engagement and performance

    o are more likely to be motivated, feel valued, grow trust and build stronger relationships.

- When you actively choose to create a positive emotional state in yourself, it positively influences the emotional state of people around you.

- The act of focusing and paying attention (e.g. to a thought, insight, activity, picture or feeling) stabilises your brain connections, which maintains your emotional state associated with that experience. Paying attention repeatedly to positive experiences makes these changes permanent so you automatically see a positive perspective. In the same way, daily practice at any speciality (playing the piano, finance, science, etc.) reshapes the pattern of connections in your brain so you interpret the world in a different way.

- Your surroundings influence your emotional state. It is worth reviewing how well:

    o your office space stimulates positive states (yes, physical space can make a difference to how well people get on with each other and work together)

    o organisational systems and processes enable people to excel at their role, rather than frustrating, delaying or blocking progress.

9. The power of positive

Take control of your self-talk

Self-talk is the mind chatter and thoughts you think throughout the day. How constructive is your self-talk? Would you accept that kind of talk from anyone else? Would you say that to your best friend? If you answer 'no' to the last two questions, why are you doing this to yourself? Raising your awareness of your self-talk gives you the opportunity to do something about it.

Positive thinking rewires your brain when you learn to focus your attention on being aware of underlying intrusive negative thoughts and consciously change them. When you observe your thoughts and feelings, you can choose to respond rationally to emotionally stressful stimuli, choose more appropriate behaviours, reduce stress, be more confident and think positively. It creates new connections in your brain, and the more you use them the stronger those connections become. After a while, you build a new, good habit of positive thinking, and stop (or almost stop) the incessant mindless negative chatter that most people discover is their predominant non-conscious mode when they first start paying attention to their self-talk.

- Pay attention to your self-talk.

- Keep a tally of negative thoughts in a notebook or app on your phone. Notice the number. Many people find just becoming mindful and aware of self-talk reduces how often they have automatic negative thoughts. Review the numbers over a week.

- Step it up and challenge negative thoughts: examine your interpretation, identify, debate and counter the underlying belief and find alternative perspectives and interpretations that are less catastrophic. Reframe to a positive thought that you can believe in.

- Review the patterns in your self-talk. Notice any particular triggering situations or environments and plan how you can prevent being triggered by breaking state. Notice how your habits of self-talk are changing as you start to take control of your mindset.

Actions to create positive mindsets and cultures

- Exercise and relaxation techniques create positive body states.
- Renewal: do at least one thing just for fun every day. Something that makes you laugh, or feel refreshed and renewed. With people or alone. What can your team do together weekly that is fun?
- Stop the amygdala hijack: break state to stop the spiralling emotions and break your thought pattern. Use a snap band on your wrist or take a deep breath and count to ten.
- Associate cues with a resourceful state, so you can call on that desired state at will. For example, a physical cue you can fire at will, a picture that reminds you of your intentions, your goal mantra to keep focus.
- Really listen and pay attention, so the person feels respected and understood (Chapter 4).
- Show appreciation and recognise people's efforts. Give specific praise and compliments. Note what you liked and what difference it makes and praise effort to develop a growth mindset. Avoid the bland and meaningless 'well done'.
- Learn to receive and accept compliments gracefully. If you find it hard, just say 'thank you' or 'you're welcome' and stop brushing it off with something like, 'Oh, it's nothing'.
- Give positive, evidence-based, constructive feedback and feedforward frequently.

- Be kind: look out for what you can do for others and give small gifts without expectation of receiving one back, for example a birthday card, cake or compliments. Acts of kindness stimulate your reward centre as well as the recipient's reward centre, making both of you feel good.

- Train yourself to notice automatically what is going well: write three things daily that went well and your part in making them happen.

- Recognise all achievements and progress: for example start every team meeting with each person reporting one thing they have done and how it contributes to progress towards priority goals; write achievements on a whiteboard on the wall.

- Make social interactions positive: for example co-create meeting/team/organisational ground rules about how we want to work together and behave with each other; when someone is new, connect with them first and make one-to-one introductions when they join the group or network (reduces 'stranger' fear, see Chapter 10).

- Celebrate achievements: know what type of celebration is meaningful for you and your team members.

- Build your confidence and your team members' confidence.

10. Understanding motivation

Motivation is vital for engagement and is defined as a driving force that initiates and directs your behaviour. The most powerful is an inner energy that makes you want to do something and spurs you into action to achieve it. That inner fire needs to be fanned into flames and nurtured to prevent it dying back to embers or going out. Understanding how motivation works through emotions can help you to design ways of working to keep your own motivation burning bright, and fire up other people's motivation to inspire them to be engaged in their work.

Extrinsic (external) vs intrinsic (internal) motivators

Think for a moment about what motivates you… and notice the language you use when you think about doing something.

- Should, must, ought to, have to, expected to, could – indicates that there is an external component. Forced, pressured, controlled or coerced has purely extrinsic motivation – you would not do it at all if the external stimulus was not there. Doing something because you feel guilty if you don't do it, or because you think it is a good thing to do, are examples of increasing self-determination in choosing to do something in response to an extrinsic motivator. Yet there

is still an element of doing it because there is some external consequence (self-determination theory; Deci, 2012).
- Love to, want to, will, enjoy, fun – indicates internal motivation and fully self-determined behaviour. You do not need any external stimulus to make you do this; you choose to do it of your own free will and out of interest.

External motivators provide external rewards or threats that drive your behaviour, including basic needs for warmth or food. These are often thought of as 'carrot and stick' motivators – for example you are paid a salary for doing work that you would not do otherwise; your wage is docked if you don't turn up on time. External rewards can lead to job dissatisfaction if they are not high enough, but are motivating beyond a base level until you have enough, beyond which they are no more motivating and may even be demotivating. Dan Pink (2011), in his book and video, *Drive*, describes salary as motivating up until you have sufficient money to cover your needs, and beyond that level it is less motivating. You need something else to give extra value in terms of your attention, time, energy, focus, quality of work and so on. However, if the external motivator is not high enough, or your basic physical and physiological needs are not met, it doesn't matter how highly positive the intrinsic rewards are, you remain dissatisfied.

Intrinsic motivators are more powerful because they reward innate, psychological needs and your behaviour is self-determined – you do something because you enjoy it or want to do it for yourself, not because someone else makes you do it, or you think you should do it. Intrinsic motivators inspire people to be personally interested in doing their work and lead to high engagement, improving people's wellbeing, job satisfaction, performance and commitment to their organisation.

In the SCARF model and other neuroscience research, Rock (2008) describes that when you get intrinsic motivators right, they stimulate the reward centres, releasing positive emotions. When you get them wrong, they stimulate the threat system so you are not motivated and may be in active avoidance mode, depending on the intensity of sensed threat to the motivator. Sometimes the threats can be subtle and not intuitive – for example giving advice in a conversation could be felt as a threat to status, a perception of being judged less than someone, or being undermined or put down, even when the speaker had intended to be helpful.

This is why it is vital to understand how motivation works when you want people to be engaged, committed to their work and perform well, even when your organisation must experience change as the world about us changes rapidly. It is well worth thinking creatively for even small and subtle ways in which you can satisfy intrinsic motivators, even within the confines of your role or situation in the workplace.

Nine core intrinsic motivators

I have identified nine core intrinsic motivators from five key theories (of the many) about motivation (Table 2).

Table 2: Nine core intrinsic motivators and basic needs: how the models relate

Motivator	Maslow: Hierarchy of needs	Hertzberg: Job satisfaction factors	David Rock: SCARF model	Dan Pink: Drive	Thomas: Four intrinsic motivators
Autonomy/ choice	5. Self-actualisation/ fulfilment	Responsibility	✓	✓	✓
Belonging/ relatedness	3. Love or belonging – by and for others		✓		
Competence/ mastery	5. Self-actualisation/ fulfilment	The work itself, growth and advancement	Status	✓	✓
Meaning/ purpose	5. Self-actualisation/ fulfilment	The work itself		✓	✓

Achievement/ progress	5. Self-actualisation/ fulfilment	✓		Status	✓
Recognition	4. Esteem – from self and others	✓		Status	
Status		Hygiene factor		✓	
Certainty				✓	
Fairness				✓	
Satisfy basic needs	2. Safety, security 1. Physical and physiological – eat, keep warm, etc.	Hygiene (job dissatisfaction) factors e.g.: pay, status, security, working conditions			

Autonomy/choice

A sense of control over one's environment, including freedom of choice, ability to influence outcomes, self-direction, self-management, responsibility and decision making. Major threats frequently found at work are micromanagement, lack of clearly defined expectations/boundaries and inability to control your own environment.

Belonging/relatedness

A sense of relatedness, including effective relationships, love, being part of a community, being in or out of a social group. Satisfying a sense of belonging promotes bonding, affiliative behaviour and collaboration, positive relationships and trust. Having a best friend at work is important for engagement (Gallup, 2013). Diversity, difference and networking can be perceived as 'unsafe social interactions' leading to discomfort.

Competence/mastery

A sense of mastery, including growth and advancement, and learning. Also see 'Status' below.

Meaning/purpose

Meaning and purpose are the most important motivators for engagement at work (see Chapter 3).

Achievement/progress

A sense of progress in achieving our purpose, tasks and so on. Maximise this by recognising all positive outcomes normally taken for granted, record achievements to visualise progress and celebrate steps.

Recognition

Recognition from others, and by ourselves, is important and may come into competence (recognition that acknowledges your competence), status that is affected by public recognition, and possibly also belonging, meaning and achievement, depending on your personal sense of recognition.

Status

Status is about relative standards, importance, 'pecking order' and seniority, and can be in comparison to yourself in the past, not necessarily with other people. This means raising your capability and expertise, and public recognition of improvements can be felt as a reward to the status motivator too. Status is often associated with power, which can be a strong motivator, but is not always the reason why all people take on responsibility. Some people step up because they want to contribute and make a difference.

Certainty

Meeting expectations, consistent behaviour, clarity on role boundaries, project schedules and updates, and familiarity with processes, events or environments can feel positive. Change and uncertainty can feel threatening, which diminishes cognitive power and hence performance. The brain is structured to analyse repeatable patterns and predict the immediate future, so it can make appropriate responses to keep you safe from danger. Rock (2008) states that when the environment around you is predictable and congruent, the part of the brain responsible for monitoring 'certainty' is quiet. However, even a small amount of uncertainty or change demands attention and distracts you from whatever it was you were doing. This means any change is experienced as pain and physiological discomfort, and you need to counteract it when your organisation or team experiences periods of change, which are inevitable as the world about us changes rapidly.

Fairness

People feel positive when actions and exchanges are fair, such as having the same rules for everyone, there is fair division of work and no favouritism. A sense of unfairness can be triggered easily and often contributes to conflict situations in the workplace.

Hope

Although not included in most motivation literature, having a sense of hope, that 'there is light at the end of the tunnel', is important to spur you on to do something and maintain momentum, especially in situations that could otherwise be overwhelming. I think hope could be linked to purpose and is also about belief that something is ultimately possible and that you will get there in the end.

Resources and references

Online resources and tools supporting this book:
engagingyourpeople.com

My blog: aeona.wordpress.com

Adair, J.E. (1973) *Action-Centred Leadership*. McGraw-Hill.

Argyris, C. (1990) *Overcoming Organizational Defenses: Facilitating organizational learning*. Prentice Hall.

Blanchard, K., Zigarmi, P. and Zigarmi, D. (1985) *Leadership and the One Minute Manager: Increasing effectiveness through situational leadership*. William Morrow.

Collins, J. (2001) *Good to Great*. Random House Business Books.

Cuddy, A. (2012) *Your body language shapes who you are*. TED Talk. Available at: https://youtu.be/Ks-_Mh1QhMc Accessed: 02/02/2017.

Deci, E. (2012) *Promoting motivation, health, and excellence*. TED Talk. Available at: https://youtu.be/VGrcets0E6I Accessed: 02/02/2017.

Dweck, C. (2012) *Growth Mindset*. Constable and Robinson Ltd.

Gallup (2013) *State of the Global Workplace*. Gallup, Inc. White Paper.

Gallwey, W.T. (2001) *The Inner Game of Work: Focus, learning, pleasure, and mobility in the workplace*. Random House Trade Paperback Edition.

Goleman, D. (2000) *Working With Emotional Intelligence*. Bantam.

Hersey P. and Blanchard K.H. (1977) *Management of Organization Behaviour: Utilizing human resources*. 3rd edn. Prentice Hall, Inc.

ILM (2014) *The Truth About Trust: Honesty and integrity at work*. Institute of Leadership and Management Research Paper.

Jeffrey, K., Mahoney, S., Michaelson, J. and Abdallah, S. (2014) *Well-being at work: A review of the literature*. New Economics Foundation White Paper.

Joyce, W., Nohria, N. and Robertson, B. (2004) *What Really Works: The 4+2 formula for sustained business success*. Collins Business.

Knight, S. (2009) *NLP at Work*. 3rd edn. Nicholas Brealey Publishing.

Kouzes, J. and Posner, B. (2012) *The Leadership Challenge.* 5th edn. Jossey-Bass.

MacLeod, D. and Clarke, N. (2009) *Engaging for Success: Enhancing performance through employee engagement*. A report to government. Department for Business, Innovation and Skills Report.

Navarro, J. (2011) *Louder Than Words*. Harper Paperback.

Pink, D. (2011) *Drive: The surprising truth about what motivates us*. Canongate Books.

PwC (2015) *An HR perspective: 2015 employee engagement landscape study: Championing greatness or capturing mediocrity*. PwC White Paper.

Rath, T. (2007) *Strengthsfinder 2.0*. Gallup Press.

Rock, D. (2008) 'SCARF: A brain-based model for collaborating with and influencing others'. *Neuro Leadership Journal* Vol. 1.

Shell, G.R. and Moussa, M. (2008) *The Art of Woo: Using persuasion to sell your ideas*. Capstone.

Strycharczyk, D. and Elvin, C. (2014) *Developing Resilient Organisations. How to create an adaptive, high-performance and engaged organisation*. Kogan Page Limited.

Strycharczyk, D., Clough, P. and Heffernan, N. (2015) 'The integrated leadership model'. In Passmore, J. (ed.), *Leadership Coaching: Working with leaders to develop elite performance*. 2nd edn. Kogan Page Limited, pp. 33–50.

Thomas, K.W. (2009) *Intrinsic Motivation at Work*. 2nd edn. Berrett-Koehler Publishers Inc.

Whitmore, J. (2002) *Coaching for Performance: Growing people, performance and purpose*. 3rd edn, Nicholas Brealey Publishing.

> Many organisations believe there is no place for emotion at work but the best organisations realise it is essential to evoke positive emotion to grow engagement and wellbeing for a sustainable high performance.

About the author

Dr Sue Mitchell is Director of Aeona, an Approved Development Provider with the Institute of Leadership and Management (ILM) for Leadership and Coaching programmes. Sue works with organisations, leaders, managers, business owners and private clients to inspire them to achieve results, make a difference and change their world for the better. Clients come from organisations of all types and size from start-ups, sole practitioners and SMEs to multinational corporates, the public sector and third sector.

Sue specialises in supporting people and organisations to work with mindset to raise personal, team and organisational performance, engagement and wellbeing. Specific topics include motivation, confidence, emotional intelligence, resilience, mental toughness, and values-driven leadership. Sue delivers executive one-on-one coaching, leadership development and other programmes. She facilitates half-day workshops to multi-day events, including ILM Development programme modules, team building and facilitated visioning and strategy sessions. Sue is a highly-rated speaker at conferences, seminars and CPD events for professional organisations.

About the author

Sue has over 20 years' experience as a trainer and coach and her practical approach is supported by academic ability and diverse knowledge. Sue's professional approach includes relevant qualifications, regular CPD (Continuing Professional Development) and membership of professional bodies [Association for Coaching (AC), Institute of Directors (IOD), ILM and Professional Speakers Association (PSA)]. Sue volunteers on the board of Women in Banking and Finance Edinburgh Branch, is chair of Moorfoot Community Council and qualified as a National Instructor with the British Sub Aqua Club in 2006. She draws on skills from her coaching and training experience and also running a business, leading adventurous and scuba diving expeditions overseas, and years of scientific research in behaviour and evolutionary ecology, to support clients to hone in on the issues, elucidate patterns, uncover assumptions and gain clarity, focus and direction.

Contact details

Email: sue@aeona.co.uk

Websites:

aeona.co.uk

confidentleader.co.uk

engagingyourpeople.com

leadersinscotland.co.uk

linkedin.com/in/suemitchell

Telephone: 0845 6436 084

Other Authority Guides

The Authority Guide to Mindful Leadership:
Simple techniques and exercises to manage yourself, manage others and effect change
Palma Michel

How do you implement mindfulness in the workplace?

Today's leaders and organisations need to develop an agile mindset and take bold risks. This *Authority Guide* shows you how to link mindfulness directly to leadership and business challenges and offers practical and accessible tools for change. Written by an expert on leadership, meditation and mindfulness, the book teaches you how to manage your inner landscape of thoughts, emotions and interruptions so that you can create a compassionate, innovative and sustainable working culture.

The Authority Guide to PR for Small Businesses:
Use the power of public relations and the media to reach your target customer and grow your business
Steve Bustin

Get media coverage and grow your business through PR with this practical guide.

Any business wanting to reach new customers should be embracing public relations to spread their key messages. If you don't, your competitors will. This *Authority Guide* shows you how to grab the headlines (for all the right reasons), reach huge audiences and grow your business by accessing the media to tell your story.

The Authority Guide to Emotional Resilience in Business: Strategies to manage stress and weather storms in the workplace
Robin Hills

How do your challenges inside and outside of work impact upon your emotions and your resilience?

The emotional resilience of those involved in a business will contribute significantly to the organisation's success. This *Authority Guide* from leading emotional intelligence expert, Robin Hills, will help you change the way you think about yourself and the way you approach potentially difficult situations. You will be able to develop your own personal resilience and understand how to develop resilience within the hearts and minds of your team and your organisation.

We hope that you've enjoyed reading this *Authority Guide*. Titles in this series are designed to offer highly practical and easily-accessible advice on a range of business, leadership and management issues.

We're always looking for new authors. If you're an expert in your field and are interested in working with us, we'd be delighted to hear from you. Please contact us at commissioning@suerichardson.co.uk and tell us about your idea for an *Authority Guide*.